**YOU CAN
HELP
MAKE IT
HAPPEN**

YOU CAN HELP MAKE IT HAPPEN

BY WILFRED BOCKELMAN

ILLUSTRATED BY
RAY BARTON

For Church Members
Who Feel Their Work
Should Be Exciting

AUGSBURG PUBLISHING HOUSE
Minneapolis, Minnesota

Presented to

_____

by

_____

in the hope
that it may help you
find joy in serving
this congregation

CONTENTS

Chapter 1: Who's You? What's It?
            And Where's It Happening? .. 13

Chapter 2: A God Big Enough to Be Exciting 19

Chapter 3: Not Everything That Applies
            to Apples and Trees
            Applies to People 27

Chapter 4: Tonsils Aren't Better Than
            an Appendix; They're Just
            Different 33

Chapter 5: There May Be Good Structure
            and Bad Structure, But There
            Is No Such Thing as
            No Structure 39

Chapter 6: Church Constitutions:
            Dams or Sluice Gates? 45

Chapter 7: Designing New Structures 55

Chapter 8: Don't Burn Down a Cathedral
            to Fry an Egg 67

Chapter 9: Getting Along with the Pastor
            and the Church at Large 75

Chapter 10: You Do It By Doing It 81

            Readings 85

FOREWORD

The church is under attack. The foundation is sound. Other foundation can no man lay than that which is laid, even Jesus Christ. Much of the superstructure has become shaky and some of it has toppled.

Forms change. Well-intentioned men are attracted to forms. It takes courage to bring in the bulldozer when forms have lost their usefulness. It is the history of the people of God that God raises up abrasive prophets and sometimes enemies to destroy the forms which have lost their content.

The foundation cannot stand empty. God raises up prophets to build, with zeal, dedication, and patience—to rebuild, renew, reform.

This is a great day for laymen in the church who want to build. In this book Wilfred Bockelman addresses himself to laymen. *You Can Help Make It Happen* is intended for those who have not given up on the institutional church, or at least are willing to give it one more try.

You Can Help Make It Happen goes on the assumption that laymen have intelligence and creativity. It gives assurance and encouragement—assurance that the church still has an exciting future as long as God continues to work through imperfect human beings to carry out his purpose, and encouragement to join those builders who have not given up hope.

Not everyone will agree with everything the author has to say about the church, with every analysis of its problems, and every solution or suggestion offered for doing something to put things right. There has been a tendency within the church to limit God to a very few modes of operation—preferably to those most of us have grown up with and found meaningful. In the attempt to fight relativism we have often resisted new structures, evidently thinking we were bearing witness to the changelessness of the gospel. The gospel does not change, structures do.

Bockelman emphasizes St. Paul's concept of the diversity of gifts expressed in 1 Corinthians 12. All Christians, even in the same congregation, are not alike. Paul says that gifts of many different varieties are used by God to accomplish his purposes. His mind is not our mind, and his ways go beyond ours.

God expresses himself in harmony and counterpoint—and at times even in dissonance—rather than in one line of familiar and often sentimental melody. Once we let the full grace of God do its work, we are free to work with fellow Christians with whom we are in basic agreement but with whom we also enjoy the creative give and take of hammering out unresolved issues as we develop differing structures for service.

You Can Help Make It Happen encourages readers to draw even closer together by drawing close to God in Christ, and it stimulates them to be creative in finding exciting ways to serve. At the same time it is realistic, recognizing that congregations move slowly and change even more slowly.

The book is stimulating for all thinking church members, particularly for those elected to councils, boards, and committees of local churches. It can be exciting to work with others in the church. Churches and church members need to share in this excitement.

Oswald C. J. Hoffmann

1

WHO'S YOU? WHAT'S IT? AND WHERE'S IT HAPPENING?

This book is written for three kinds of people:

1. Those who have just been elected to a committee, board, or council in your church and are perhaps a bit bewildered about their new responsibility, but are also determined to have the experience be a meaningful one. (Church here means local congregation and not a city, state, or national ecclesiastical body.)

2. Those who may already be on such a committee or board but are wondering whether it's really worth their time and effort. This book is intended to provide stimulation that will inject new life and excitement into church committees.

3. Those who are not members of any board or committee in a church **but would like to be.** The idea that it is legitimate for someone actively to seek election to a church board — or at least have a desire to serve on such a board — may come as a surprise to some people. In the first place, there are many who think that this would be the most boring assignment anyone could have, and who

would want it? Others are still victims of a false sense of modesty and humility, even to the extent of feeling that they have to vote against themselves if nominated for a church office, because voting for oneself would be unseemly.

If you belong in one of these three categories, you are the "you" referred to in the title of this book. While it is not intended to give you ideas on how to develop a campaign strategy to get elected to the top board of your church (if you belong to the third category listed above), it will give suggestions on how to become involved in action in other ways.

And that takes us to the **it** in the title—*You Can Help Make It Happen*. What is that **it** that's supposed to happen? Some people may even be surprised to find out that something is really supposed to happen in church. We have often had an image of the church as being a stabilizing influence in life. It's the world that's upsetting. We go to church to find respite, to be calmed down. The very architecture—stained glass windows and vaulted ceilings—inspires quietness. Even the double fortissimo thunder of the organ is intended for reflection rather than for action.

We whistle in the dark to assure ourselves of the power of the gospel by quoting from the book of Acts that the apostles turned the world upside down. But for the most part the words are empty rhetoric. We're uncomfortable with those who indeed would like to turn the world upside down.

And yet, anyone living in the 70s is aware that the church is under severe criticism for not being active enough. "Why go to church? Nothing ever happens there," is a common complaint.

For the moment, we will go on the assumption that something is supposed to happen at church.

We'll go on the further assumption that not only would you like to see something happen in your church, but that **you can help** make it happen. This "it" that we're talking about could perhaps best be described in the experience of a retired executive vice president of a large oil company.

"I never really found in the church the same exhilaration I found in business," he said. "I was fascinated by my job. My associates and I tackled problems together, and when we were successful in solving them, there was a sense of excitement and enthusiasm that made life worth living. But my church activity was on the periphery of my real life, where the action and excitement was taking place.

"I went to church because my wife and children liked the associations there; and I did think that there might come a day when I would really need the church. So I went — even rather regularly — but I can't honestly say that it made a deep impact on my life."

When he retired, he and his wife moved to a southern city and began looking for a church. They found one that belonged to a well-known denomination. It had a good choir, a good preacher, attractive architecture. The important people of town went there.

"We almost made the mistake of joining that church," said the retired executive. "Then we discovered a small house church in the community — a group of people that met in homes for worship. They were an alive and exciting group. They had a sense of mission and weren't afraid to take some risks. This was the church we joined, and for the first time in my life I found the same excitement and exhilaration in my church that I had formerly felt in my business."

He is convinced that that same type of excitement could happen in well-established congregations in traditional denominations.

This book is written in the conviction that you could help make the same kind of excitement happen in your church.

2
A GOD BIG ENOUGH TO BE EXCITING

You would hardly allow yourself to be nominated to a board of a company or become associated with a business without knowing something of its purpose. To serve with integrity as a member of the highest elective board of a congregation it is hardly enough to have your knowledge of the church limited to a general feeling that the church is against sin.

And if you feel that your knowledge of the church and what it stands for is inadequate, you have only two choices left open to you: either determine to learn more about it or resign. If you think that's rather blunt, you are correct. There really is no other alternative.

Note well, however, that the above paragraph does not say that you have to know all there is to know; nor does it specify how much you have to know, but only that you are determined to learn.

At the risk of insulting your intelligence, let's begin with the basic, simple fact that the church has something to do with the relationship of the individual to God and to other people.

If you feel uncomfortable talking about God, you probably have a lot of company. Some people have the kind of personality that just seems to make it easy for them to talk about God, the church, and things religious. This book is not intended to make you gregarious so that you can talk freely about religion, God, or the church to any stranger you meet — or even your friends. Some people are just wired up differently than others. We don't want to fall victim to the fallacy of judging a person's Christianity by the ease with which he can talk freely about spiritual matters.

At the same time, you will grant it is a bit strange if a business man is always reluctant or finds it extremely difficult to talk about his business. One of the purposes of this book is to get you to feel as exhilarated about your church as you do — or feel you should be — about your business. The experience of the oil company executive in the first chapter can be yours. Participating in the work of the church can be exciting.

One reason many people feel uncomfortable talking about God is that they have a guilt complex. They may have been brought up on a negative feeling about God. God has always been a big no-no to them. God is a strict master whom they have offended, and so they are always in an awkward and uneasy relationship with him.

The basic teaching of the gospel presents a totally different image of God. The doctrine of grace and forgiveness forms the basis of a relationship with God. He accepts you as you are. You don't have to reach some kind of difficult-to-achieve standard first before God accepts you.

A theological phrase on which many of us grew up was "law and gospel" — and in that order. Law confronted the individual with the demands of

God. Gospel brought forgiveness to men who could not live up to the demands of God. So far, so good. That's sound theology, but the insistence that they always have to come in that order often left some unwholesome aftereffects. One of these aftereffects is described by another phrase—"hell-fire and brimstone."

Some preachers felt that the best way to magnify the greatness of God's love was to first emphasize his wrath over broken commandments. The theory was that the more a person became convinced of his sinfulness, the more he would appreciate the love of God.

Human nature being what it is, what comes first is usually thought of as being the more important. Once you have been indoctrinated with the "law and gospel" phrase, the burden of proof becomes quite heavy to show that the second is really more important than the first.

The fact is that gospel really precedes law. It's unfortunate that in the presentation of the Ten Commandments, some catechisms leave out an important clause that is in the Exodus account. The introduction to the Commandments as given in some catechisms is simply: "I am the Lord thy God. Thou shalt have no other gods before me."

The Exodus account, however, reads, "I am the Lord your God, **who brought you out of the land of Egypt, out of the house of bondage.** You shall have no other gods before me."

Undoubtedly those who produced some catechisms concluded that the reference to Egypt really doesn't apply to today's situation. In removing it, however, they de-emphasized a very important part, namely that gospel precedes law.

The people of Israel had already had a gospel encounter with God before he gave the law. He didn't give them the commandments first and then tell them that if they kept these he would free them. This progression of events has some important implications for the individual's relationship with God. God doesn't insist that you first reach a certain standard of obedience before he accepts you. This is what the gospel is all about — that you need not have a guilt complex and feel that a relationship with God is awkward and embarrassing. Not only does the gospel remove embarrassment, but it adds a dimension of excitement and exhilaration.

A book highly recommended to church leaders who want a larger vision of God is *Your God Is Too Small*, by J. B. Phillips. In the introduction to the book, Phillips writes:

> *The trouble with many people today is that they have not found a God big enough for modern needs. While their experience of life has grown in a score of directions, and their mental horizons have been expanded to the point of bewilderment by world events and by scientific discoveries, their ideas of God have remained largely static.*

"Many men and women are living, often with inner dissatisfaction, without any faith in God at all," says Phillips. "This is not because they are particularly wicked or selfish, or, as the old-fashioned would say, 'godless,' but because they have not found with their adult minds a God big enough to 'account for' life, big enough to 'fit in with' the new scientific age, big enough to command their highest admiration and respect, and consequently their willing cooperation."

A tendency of the traditional Christian is to be reluctant to think new thoughts about God for fear that his new expressions may be "too liberal."

One of the great tragedies of some fundamentalist churches is that while in theory they believe in salvation by grace, in practice they act as though they believe in salvation by having the right answers. Since laymen often feel theologically insecure they are either hesitant to hold an opinion firmly or else they are very reluctant to change a position once taken for fear they may be making a mistake.

Martin Luther had a motto that should be a great boon to such people. "Sin bravely," said Luther. By this he did not mean to go out on an orgy or to paint the town ten shades of red.

What he meant to say was that the very nature of being human means that you've got to have opinions and make decisions. Sometimes you would rather not make decisions, for the chances for making mistakes are pretty overwhelming. You would rather wait until all the facts are in. But **all** the facts probably never will be in.

To the Christian in this situation Luther says, in effect: Sin bravely. Don't keep from having opinions or making decisions because you're afraid you may make a mistake. Making a mistake won't damn you. That's what grace is for—to forgive you when you make a mistake.

To one who has experienced this forgiveness, it will never again be a cliché to say that the gospel liberates. Reduced to two words, the gospel says, "Fear not." And to proclaim the gospel means to announce to people, "Don't be afraid." Those few words have many implications, and a lifetime will be too short to explore them all. But they do provide the basis for an exciting relationship with God.

You may still have the nagging feeling that there must be a catch somewhere. You recall hearing something about repentance, with a strong implication of **if**—**if** you feel sorry for your sins, **if** you repent and turn to God, **then** God will accept you. But your problem is you're never quite sure when you have repented enough, when you have been sorry enough to pass the test to have God accept you.

Let's say it again: gospel precedes law. John the Baptist in announcing the beginning of the Lord's ministry did not say, "Repent and the kingdom of God **will come.**" Instead, he said, "Repent for the kingdom of God **is at hand.**"

There is plenty of room for repentance, but it is not so much a condition under which God accepts you into the kingdom as it is a discipline that enriches your life in the kingdom by challenging you to move from where you are to what you can become.

One of the paradoxes of the Christian faith is that you become what you already are. A baby is a person the day he is born. At the same time, he becomes more of a person every day. He doesn't have to achieve certain things first before he becomes a person. Upon the death of a king, the oldest son is king even though he is only a day old, but years of training cause him to become more of what he already is.

This view of our relationship with God is not to say that there will be no problems, even for the Christian, but it is to say that there will be excitement even in the solving of the problems, for we know that God gives us the resources to solve problems.

If you feel that words such as excitement and exhilaration have appeared rather often in this chapter, you are correct. John Wesley used to say, "Why should the devil have all the good tunes?" Too often Christianity has been altogether too glum. But neither are we impressed with a perpetual, artificial saccharine smile or a self-generated, bubbly effervescence, if that is the only alternative to glumness.

But the Christian can walk with a strong, positive stride and assurance that along with other Christians he can make things happen. A person elected to a committee or board in the church is blessed because he has more opportunity to help make it happen.

3

NOT
EVERYTHING
THAT APPLIES TO APPLES
AND TREES
APPLIES TO PEOPLE

Earlier in this book we learned that basically and essentially "the church has something to do with the relationship of the individual to God and to other people." The previous chapter dealt with the relationship of the individual with God. This one will deal with the relationship of the individual with other people.

For the traditional Christian there will always be the temptation to insist that in point of time the right relationship between the individual and God must come first. Then from this, the right relationship between the individuals will come about automatically. But it is not necessarily so.

To insist on this progression of attitude to action as the only acceptable one would mean that a proper relationship with God could be established in a vacuum, or at least apart from people, and then transplanted into a people situation, with the guarantee that it will work there.

This approach takes for granted that faith produces good works, that a correct attitude toward God automatically results in correct behavior toward fellowmen. To get good behavior, first get the right attitude. It's the old argument of "a good tree brings forth good fruit." And from this argument follows the analogy that simply to tie good apples on a dead apple tree will not bring the tree back to life. Nor will it keep the apples from rotting. But as with all analogies, so with this one too: it limps. Don't push the point too far.

Not everything that applies to apples and trees applies to people. Another school of thought holds that changed behavior **can result** in change of attitude. In other words, it is possible for a person to be encouraged to change his behavior toward people and this can result in a change of attitude toward people and even toward God.

For purposes of analysis and understanding it is helpful to distinguish between the two relationships, but it is impossible to separate them. Faith in God is created on a stage peopled with fellow human beings. A church must do both: be concerned about nurturing a person's faith in God and at the same time make possible a growing relationship with people. There is no hard and fast rule that you must always begin with the same one. In fact there are times when a close relationship with fellow members of a church can lead to a deeper relationship with God.

The Apostle John makes two statements about relationships between Christians that at first glance seem paradoxical. In Chapter 13 of his Gospel, he writes, "By this shall all men know that you are my disciples if you have love for one another." Two chapters later he says, "This I command you, to love one another."

On the one hand, why should it be so surprising that Christians should love each other? Shouldn't that be expected? Why should that make such an impression on people? One might be surprised if a person loved his enemies; and at another point Christ did say that one of the marks of a Christian is that he loves his enemies. But here in John's Gospel he is quoted as saying that the most powerful witness Christians can give to the world is that they love one another.

And on the other hand, what kind of love is it if it has to be commanded? Can it indeed be love at all? But the more we think about these two passages the more we see the realism of Christ. Often it is easier to love strangers or even enemies with whom one has only fleeting contact — and that often at times of their best behavior — than it is to love people with whom you have close associations and whose company you share when the behavior of either, you or them, is less than ideal. To really love takes discipline. It doesn't always come naturally. It must be worked at. But it is worth more than the effort it takes. And those who have experienced the richness of fellowship with other Christians have also experienced the richness of fellowship that they have had with God. Why have a philosophical debate over which must come first?

We go back again to the oil company executive mentioned in the first chapter. He found a relationship with God exciting because he had found an exciting relationship with other Christians.

No matter how strongly your church may emphasize a correct, doctrinal understanding of God and the Bible, if it does not put equal emphasis on a living relationship among its members, it will be joyless and unattractive. The most exciting and attractive church is still the one about whom others will say — as they said of the first Christians — "Behold how they love one another."

One of the greatest blessings you will experience as a member of a church board or committee will be your relationship with other people committed to the same cause. There is no guarantee that this relationship will automatically be a good one. There can be strong differences of opinion among members of a church board just as there can be in politics. And these differences can at times express themselves in outright bitterness. But differences of opinion can also have a strong positive potential, as will be pointed out in the next chapter. You can help make it happen.

4

TONSILS AREN'T
BETTER THAN
AN APPENDIX
THEY'RE JUST
DIFFERENT

Every member of a church board or committee ought to read 1 Corinthians 12 and 13 at least once a month. Perhaps the best time would be just before going to your meeting or just after returning, to remind yourself that it is not necessary that everybody always agree on everything. Most people are acquainted with 1 Corinthians 13. It's Paul's great love chapter that begins with the eloquent words, "If I speak in the tongues of men and of angels, but have not love, I am a noisy gong or a clanging cymbal," and closes with the equally eloquent words, "So faith, hope, love abide, these three; but the greatest of these is love."

But the preceding chapter is equally powerful and is particularly meaningful to people who work together with other people in the church. Phillips translates part of that chapter as follows:

> As the human body, which has many parts, is a unity, and those parts, despite their multiplicity, constitute one single body, so it is with Christ. For we were all baptized by the Spirit into one body, whether we were Jews, Greeks,

slaves, or free men, and we have all had experience of the same Spirit.

Now the body is not one member but many. If the foot should say, "Because I am not a hand I don't belong to the body," does that alter the fact that the foot IS a part of the body? Or if the ear should say, "Because I am not an eye I don't belong to the body," does that mean that the ear really is not part of the body? After all, if the body were all one eye, for example, where would be the sense of hearing? Or if it were all one ear, where would be the sense of smell? But God has arranged all the parts in the one body, according to his design. For if everything were concentrated in one part, how could there be a body at all? The fact is there are many parts, but only one body. So that the eye cannot say to the hand, "I don't need you," nor, again, can the head say to the feet, "I don't need you!" On the contrary, those parts of the body which have no obvious function are the more essential to health; and to those parts of the body which seem to us to be less deserving of notice we have to allow the highest honor of function. The parts which do not look beautiful have a deeper beauty in the work they do, while the parts which look beautiful may not be at all essential to life! But God has harmonized the whole body by giving importance of function to the parts which lack apparent importance, that the body should work together as a whole with all the members in sympathetic relationships with one another.

There is a tendency for people to think that this world would be a wonderful place if everybody agreed on everything. It's equally logical for them to assume that if they are right in their opinion — and for the moment let's assume that they are right—then the more people they can get to agree with them, the better.

But life isn't quite that simple. At times there can be real strength in tension. The only way action is accomplished is through tension. The only reason you can raise your arm steadily is because one muscle is pulling against another muscle. This is not to suggest that there should always be strong opposition on every issue brought before a church board or committee, but it is to suggest that there can be wholesome tension. Two equally intelligent and dedicated people may hold opposite views on the best way a given task may be accomplished and from this wholesome encounter of two views may come a better and more creative way of solving a problem than if one view had gone unchallenged.

One need not shy away from the fact that there are tensions and contradictions in life. Dr. Sidney Rand, president of St. Olaf College, expresses it this way, "One of the marks of an educated man is to be able to live with unresolved issues." Reinhold Niebuhr once said, "The unfolding historical situation produces a profusion of facts, some of them contradictory to each other."

A committee in which there is no honest encounter of ideas challenging each other will not only very likely be unproductive; it will probably also be dull. It will be like a piece of music with everything written in melody, lacking the vibrancy that comes from harmony and counterpoint, or like a piece of art, all in one color.

Nor is it necessary that judgment always be expressed on whether one idea is more important than the other. Using Paul's analogy of 1 Corinthians 12, who is to say whether an eye is more important than an ear. Tonsils aren't better than an appendix; they're just different. Various organs of the body perform different functions, all of them important for the proper functioning of the body. This insight lays the groundwork for the healthy functioning of a church committee composed of members with different talents each bringing different insights to a problem.

A guide for developing one's own attitude in relation to others on a committee might well be these words from the 13th chapter of Paul's first epistle to the Corinthians:

> *This love of which I speak is slow to lose patience—it looks for a way of being constructive. It is not possessive: it is neither anxious to impress nor does it cherish inflated ideas of its own importance.*
>
> *Love has good manners and does not pursue selfish advantage. It is not touchy. It does not keep account of evil or gloat over the wickedness of other people. On the contrary, it is glad with all good men when truth prevails.*
>
> *Love knows no limit to its endurance, no end to its trust, no fading of its hope; it can outlast anything. It is, in fact, the one thing that still stands when all else has fallen* (Phillips).

Recognizing that different people bring different talents to a task and that this is a part of God's plan also says something about God. He brings richness through diversity. Earlier in the book we stressed the doctrine of grace and of the precedence of gospel over law. God does not demand that everyone be homogenized into one mass of look-alikes. He accepts people where they are, and affirms each one's individuality. When these individuals, committed to Christ, interact with each other as members of a church council, exciting things can happen. You can help make it happen.

5

THERE MAY BE
GOOD STRUCTURE
AND BAD STRUCTURE
BUT THERE IS
NO SUCH THING AS
NO STRUCTURE

We are getting to the point in the book where we will deal with some very practical aspects of board and committee business. Until now we have dealt largely with theory and with the general attitude of a committee or board member in his relationship with God as well as with other people. As we now consider the practical implication of all of this, the key word is structure. What are the mechanics by which we now put our theory into actual practice and get the job of the church done?

Structure became a kind of dirty word in the last half of the sixties. It was common to say, "I accept Christ, but I reject the church." Recognizing that this was nonsense the avant-garde Christian would often add, "What I mean is that I reject the institutional church."

But that also is nonsense. There is no such thing as Christianity or church without some structure through which it can express itself. There may be good structure and bad structure but there is no such thing as no structure.

One of the basic doctrines of the Christian faith is the doctrine of the incarnation. This doctrine says that God has tied himself to his earthly creation. The high point of the incarnation was when God himself became man through Christ. The writing of the Bible is another example of incarnation. God used human beings, their gifts of memory, imagination, personality, insight, and ability to express themselves to give us the Bible. The Apostle Paul describes them as "earthen vessels" through which God brings us spiritual treasures.

Likewise the church. It is the body of Christ, but it expresses itself in human institutions as Christians organize structures through which they get their task done. Let's not be so surprised by weaknesses and imperfections of the church. They are there by definition.

Traditionally, the 6th chapter of Acts is cited as the first reference to a church council or committee. The first seven verses of that chapter are often read when there is a formal installation of a church council. This section describes a problem that had developed in the early church regarding the care of widows. Since most of the early Christians came from Hebrew background, the widows of Greek background complained that favoritism was being shown to the Hebrew widows. The apostles were kept so busy refereeing the dispute that they had little time to do what they felt was their main task — preaching and teaching.

So we read in Acts 6:2-4: "And the twelve summoned the body of the disciples and said, 'It is not right that we should give up preaching the word of God to serve tables. Therefore, brethren, pick out from among you seven men of good repute, full of the Spirit and of wisdom, whom we may appoint to this duty. But we will devote ourselves to prayer and to the ministry of the word.' "

It may come as a surprise to those who have a very lofty image of the spiritual duties of a church council to learn that this very mundane situation gave rise to what we traditionally consider a forerunner of today's church councils. The first Christians were merely devising a structure with which to do their task.

It is interesting to note that it is usually this part of the 6th chapter of Acts that is read at installations of church councils today, and not the last part of the 4th chapter and the beginning of the 5th chapter. For they also tell the story of a structure the early Christians formed to meet a need. The only problem with that one was that it was a colossal failure.

It was the Christian's experiment with a communal style of life. Luke describes it in Acts: "There was not a needy person among them, for as many as were possessors of lands or houses sold them and brought the proceeds of what was sold and laid it at the apostles' feet; and distribution was made to each as any had need."

It was because this structure turned out less than successful that the Acts 6 account describes a new structure — the naming of seven deacons to administer a welfare program. This organizational system was probably better than the former one, but quite likely it was not perfect either.

In fact there are those today who say that this organizational structure was really quite bad too. It may have been responsible for dividing the work of the church into its two main aspects that are still in tension today — preaching, teaching, and meditation on the one hand, and action on the other. It may also account for the fact that even today in many circles there is reluctance on the part of clergymen to trust laymen with spiritual decisions.

We shouldn't call it blasphemy to at least raise the question whether the organizational structure that the disciples set up might not have been as good as we generally suppose. And if it was bad, the sin is not theirs but rather ours if we slavishly adopt a structure that may have served a purpose at one time but that has outlived its usefulness. The lesson we have to learn is that structure itself is not bad. There is no such thing as a church working without a structure.

The challenge facing church council and committee members is to develop a structure that will work in our day. Every church has some kind of constitution that spells out orderly procedures of how the church and its elected officials should do their work. Constitutions can be valuable also because they often act as a check on hastily conceived ideas, which if put into practice could be disastrous. But if we become slaves of a constitution and never ask whether it needs updating or even whether some of its basic assumptions should be challenged, then we can become a dead church.

Congregational constitutions can sometimes also be a most effective instrument to make hypocrites out of people or at least demean their faith, the very thing they are meant to enhance. Some denominations provide their congregations with model constitutions that go way back in history and subscribe to the historic statements of faith in that denomination.

The constitution of a traditional Lutheran church, for example, would contain a statement of faith subscribing to the three ecumenical creeds (the Apostles' Creed, the Nicene Creed, and the Athanasian Creed) and to the Augsburg Confession, Luther's Small and Large Catechism, the Smalcald Articles, and the Formula of Concord. Most Christians would know the Apostles' Creed. With help they could struggle through the Nicene Creed. They will remember something of their catechism and will remember having heard of the Augsburg Confession. But they probably don't have the foggiest notion of what the Athanasian Creed, the Smalcald Articles, and the Formula of Concord are.

That raises some serious questions. Should a Lutheran's integrity be questioned if he as a member of a Lutheran Church subscribes to doctrinal statements in a constitution that he has never read? Should those who devised this system of having a historical article of faith in a constitution be chastised for encouraging irresponsibility by suggesting to members that they really just take their pastor's word for the soundness of these statements? If it is so important to have statements of faith in the constitution, why is it not equally important to insist that those who subscribe to the constitution should know what it is all about? Is there perhaps some ground for the church's reputation for irrelevance? Or should the whole question of having that kind of constitution in the first place be called into question?

What is the purpose of a constitution? For that, the next chapter.

6

CHURCH CONSTITUTIONS: DAMS OR SLUICE GATES?

If the purpose of a constitution is to establish rules and regulations within which an organization carries out its duties, then the first obvious question is, what is the purpose of the organization? What is its duty?

We have already emphasized the importance of flexibility and diversity, but beneath this diversity there also needs to be a basic unifying purpose. The Bible describes the church as the body of Christ. The 12th chapter of 1 Corinthians also uses the analogy of the body and the various organs of the body, each with a different function, yet working together with others to achieve one purpose.

The major purpose of the church expresses itself in two ways, each in tension with the other. One is directed inward, nurturing the faith of those within the church. The other is directed outward, serving the world. Whenever the church gets tired of struggling with this tension and settles for the ease of living with only one of its two major responsibilities, death sets in. Tension is the law of life. The peace offered by the gospel is not a release from the tension between the inner nurture and outward service, but rather the assurance that this necessary tension is indeed the stuff of life and that it can be as exciting as life itself.

Christians will always be tempted to avoid tension and so they will attempt to keep the two separate: **first** give all attention to inner nurture **and then** to outward service. It's something like an educational program in which you first learn something in the classroom and then go out and put it into practice. But life isn't like that. It's more like a laboratory in which working and learning take place at the same time.

The two cannot be separated, but for the sake of understanding each function better, let's consider them individually. Traditionally we are probably most at home with that function of the church that deals with our nurture. The very architecture of the church emphasizes this function. We speak of "the church and education unit." We worship and teach — or are taught. In most instances the building stands empty for six days a week. It's the place we gather on Sunday to have our inner resources strengthened. The following statement of purpose and aim taken from an actual constitution of a congregation is illustrative of how virtually our total structure is aimed at carrying out this one aspect of the church's task:

> The purpose of this congregation is to provide for the Divine Word and Sacraments, free course to the mind and heart, that the Kingdom of God may come.
>
> (a) It seeks this end by diligent use of the Means of Grace in public teaching and worship.
>
> (b) To this end it also exhorts its mem-

bers to cultivate family worship that the Word of God may dwell richly among them; and, to be diligent in good works that the life of faith may be strengthened and the Kingdom extended.

The same constitution lists the following as the duties of pastor:

It is required of the pastor that he shall proclaim the revealed Word of God in all its truth and purity, and that he shall diligently and conscientiously take charge of the proper indoctrination of confirmands, as well as the instruction in general of our most holy faith, as also the spiritual care and comfort of the sick, sorrowing, tempted, dying—teaching and admonishing every member of the congregation in all that is essential for his soul's salvation.

The pastor is the shepherd of the Congregation and the congregation pledges itself to gladly accept the doctrine, exhortation, judgment, consolation, and encouragement of the Word of God from him; and look to him for all ministerial acts; manifest to him due reverence, obedience and love as the Lord, through his Holy Apostles, demands from his congregation.

These two paragraphs are then followed by six sections under the same article that deal with the calling of a pastor, his resignation, deposal, dismissal, calling of assistants, and the size vote required to effect any of these.

Absolutely the only reference in the twelve pages of this constitution to any outward service obligation of the congregation is this statement in one of the bylaws:

> *Life and Growth Committee. This committee shall be charged with the specific* duties of welfare, *music, publicity, membership, visitation,* synodical and other benevolences.

A standard letter of call one denomination uses for calling all of its pastors lists the following 14 duties of a pastor:

> *(1) Preach and teach the Word of God as revealed in the Old and New Testaments and as witnessed by the confessions of [name of denomination];*
>
> *(2) Administer the Sacraments, i.e., Holy Baptism and the Lord's Supper, according to the practice of the [name of denomination] and recommended liturgies of [denomination];*
>
> *(3) Instruct the children of the parish in the Christian faith and teach them to observe all things Christ commanded;*
>
> *(4) Minister to all the members of the parish according to their particular needs, call on them in their homes, and administer the Means of Grace to them;*
>
> *(5) Lead us in fulfilling our parish responsibility to witness for Christ and to enlist in active membership in his church all in the community who are not actively affiliated with a Christian congregation;*
>
> *(6) Attend meetings of the congregation, church council, and boards, and give pastoral leadership therein;*
>
> *(7) Oversee the work of the schools,*

organizations, and activities within the parish;

(8) Keep your practice in harmony with the Word of God, the Confessions of the [denomination] the constitution and bylaws of [denomination] and the constitution of the congregation;

(9) Conduct regular services as agreed upon by congregation and pastor;

(10) Record promptly and properly all baptisms, confirmations, marriages, funerals, and attendance at the Lord's Supper; and report the statistics of the parish promptly and fully, as required by [name of denomination];

(11) Strive in word and deed to be a worthy example in Christian living, avoiding conduct which might endanger the faith of others;

(12) Stimulate and encourage the members of the parish to support all the work of [name of denomination];

(13) Participate in the pension plan of [name of denomination];

(14) Subscribe to the Constitution and Bylaws of [name of denomination] and to the Constitution and Bylaws of the congregation.

In a few instances in this letter of call there is a remote suggestion of service. For instance, implied in the first statement—preach and teach the Word of God—there is certainly opportunity to emphasize the call to service as the Bible itself teaches. In the third statement—teaching children to observe all things Christ commanded—there is also opportunity to emphasize the service that Christ commanded. And in the fifth statement—witnessing for Christ—

there is the possibility of service, but even here it seems to have an ulterior motive, "to enlist them in active membership" in the church. That is indeed a way of serving, but would we be just as willing to continue serving if there seemed to be no prospect of getting them into church membership?

The purpose for quoting from this letter of call and from the congregational constitution is not to be critical of what these include, **but rather of what they do not include.** This does not say that these churches do not believe in what they have not included or only implied in their constitution or letter of call. It's quite probable that they feel that if there is inner growth, service to others will follow automatically.

Theoretically they are probably saying that it's not an either-or, either nurture or service; but both-and, both nurture and service. In practice, however, they are saying the one is so important that we have to be formally structured for it by constitution and letter of call, while the other will kind of take care of itself.

It's just as possible—though perhaps not quite as likely—for the reverse to happen, for a congregation to be constitutionally structured to serve, but with little or no emphasis on proper nurture in the faith. And these congregations would be as likely to say "We take that for granted," as the other congregations take service for granted. The idea is—in theory and in fact, in constitution and in practice—to emphasize both, inner growth and outward service and to hold the two in creative tension.

For the person who would like to find more excitement in his duties as a member of a church council or committee, the trend of thought is taking this direction:

1. The church as a body of Christ has a two-fold

purpose: to nurture the faith of the members of the church and to minister to the world. The Gospels are particularly emphatic about our special obligation to the poor. One cannot read the life of Christ without being impressed over and over again with the attention he paid to the poverty-stricken and the unfortunate. The church as the body of Christ can hardly be less concerned about them.

The 25th chapter of Matthew gives a graphic picture of the last judgment and the standards by which people will be judged. These standards are particularly severe when we try to justify ourselves by saying, "Our chief task was to preach the gospel and we did that."

Is it possible that Christ may say to us: "I was hungry and you gave me no food, I was thirsty and you gave me no drink, I was a stranger and you did not welcome me, naked and you did not clothe me, sick and in prison and you did not visit me. . . . Truly I say to you, as you did it not to one of the least of these, you did it not to me."

2. The church needs some structure to carry out its task. It's nonsense to say, "I accept Christianity and Christ but reject the institutional church." It's part of the doctrine of the incarnation that Christ works through some form of structure.

3. This structure has traditionally been defined in constitutions of church bodies and congregations. Church constitutions have been noted for providing a strong structure to carry out one of the purposes of the church, the inner nurture of its members. They have been notably weak in providing a structure that would enable the church to serve the community.

Perhaps the biggest challenge facing local church leaders today is to develop a structure that will enable the church to serve the community as well as it has served its own members. A constitution does not need to be dull; it can be exciting. It is not so much a dam that grudgingly holds back tons of ideas, which become stagnant. It is rather a sluice gate and a channel through which enthusiasm could surge to turn the dynamo.

You, Mr. Council or Committee Member, can help make it happen.

7

DESIGNING NEW STRUCTURES

It's always dangerous to speak of new structures, for it often turns out that what we describe as new is hundreds of years old. For instance the "new" thing in the church is to emphasize small groups and services in homes, but anyone who reads his New Testament at all gains the strong impression that this was the way the early Christians always worshiped.

Nothing is good or bad because it is old or because it is new. Human nature is such that if the old is kept too long, we get into a rut. But to adopt the new just for the sake of having something new is not the mark of intelligent action either. Because an old idea that was discarded comes back to usefulness again does not mean it should not have been discarded in the first place. Nor is it reason for a gloating "I told you so." Ideas go through cycles of death and resurrection. Our task is to get acquainted with the life cycle.

The purpose of this chapter is not to suggest that everything old should be dropped in favor of something new. It is rather to stimulate your thinking by introducing some new ideas that have been tried in some churches and have been found successful. That does not mean that they will be successful in your church. The fact of life may be that even though they might be successful, your members may not be ready for them at this time. (The next chapter will suggest ways of bridging the gap between those who seem to move too slowly and those who seem to move too fast.)

Intelligent planning should take into account the insights of church leaders who have read the pulse of the church for years and whose opinions about where the church is going are worth listening to. Before laying specific plans for your congregation's future, it would at least be interesting to take a look at the broad trend of the future as predicted by some church leaders. Following is a list of such predictions for the next quarter century as made by Roland W. Tapp:

> The church is going to have to go through the fundamentalist-liberal fight of fifty years ago all over again, with greater polarization.
>
> At practical levels there will be a growing trend toward mergers with Catholics; but the cooperation will be between fundamentalists of both groups and between liberals.
>
> The church will interest only people whose "psychological age" is about forty-five years and up.
>
> Total church membership will decrease, but those remaining will be more knowledgeable and committed.
>
> More people—not all necessarily Christians —will believe that the Christian's primary concern is with social action.
>
> Most church school teachers will see their functions as "fellow-seekers" with their students.

There will be no more denominational Christian education programs.

There will be no more projects for building huge church plants.

Integration of all minorities will become a fact in the churches.

The churches will give up their tax-exempt status.

Foreign missions will be less emphasized, probably replaced by Peace Corps types of action.

Lay academies will rise in number.

Denominational theological seminaries operating without reference to university level education will decline.

Theology will shift from transcendence and immanence to pantheism (which holds that God is everything).

Sermons are out, and so is the Sunday morning worship service.

College students and young adults will show increasing interest in religion and specifically in Christianity.

Fellowship devices will be less help in attracting new members to local churches.

There will be less interest in separate men's and women's programs, and some people will belong to more than one church.

TV will be used in church school teaching by clusters of churches in an area.

Breakdown of authority, both personal and doctrinal, will be more evident.

The church stands in very great danger of losing the intellectual elite of this country.

Resurgent interest in formal worship is only momentary.

The Church A.D. 2000 will not be recognizable by anyone today.

Not all churchmen would agree with all of these

predictions. Some of the forecasts may describe fads that may be popular for a time but will not be adequate for the foundation of a whole church program or structure. It does seem that for the present—and a considerable distance into the future—huge investments in church buildings are out. A church planning a new cathedral-like structure had better at least give it a second thought.

The prediction that "sermons are out, and so is the Sunday morning worship service" has been gaining ground. But until someone comes along with a good, strong alternative, a majority of churches will continue to have the Sunday morning worship experience as the central point of congregational life.

Nevertheless, church councils would do well to at least study the implications of predictions like these: the churches will give up their tax-exempt status; the total membership will decrease, but those remaining will be more knowledgeable and committed; the church stands in very great danger of losing the intellectual elite of this country.

The progressive churches of the future are going to change their methods of measuring their effectiveness. The new methods will be more difficult to apply than the old ones, but they will be more in line with the criteria set down in the Bible. One of the problems in the past has been that too many churches have changed the means of grace into the goals of grace.

"Means of grace" is a theological term that refers to the Word of God and the sacraments. These are the means that the church uses to do its task. And if these means are used properly, they should result in something which Paul describes in Galatians 5:22 as the fruit of the Spirit. He lists this fruit as "love, joy, peace, patience, kindness, goodness, faithfulness, gentleness, self-control." The problem with these is that they are difficult to measure. And so we have measured what was easier to measure—attendance at church and Sunday school and frequency of participation in the Lord's Supper. These we can count. Our goal often was to get the largest number of people into our churches, without considering too seriously whether this was indeed the most effective way of bringing the means of grace to them. In this vicious circle of playing the numbers game we got more people to come to church, so we had to build bigger churches, so we needed more people and more money to pay for them.

It finally dawned on us that building large church buildings and getting a lot of people into them once a week may not be the most effective way of producing the fruit of the Spirit Paul talks about. That's why Roland Tapp predicts that in the next 25 years there will be no more projects for building huge church plants. We have discovered that "love, joy, peace, patience, kindness, goodness, faithfulness, gentleness and self-control" can perhaps be better cultivated in small, highly-disciplined groups. A church that still gears all of its thinking to how to have the largest possible attendance on Sunday morning on the assumption that this almost automatically produces the fruit of the Spirit may be in danger of confusing means of grace with goals of grace. A congregation that has 90 or 100 percent of its members in church every Sunday still needs to ask the question whether it is ministering effectively, and to ask that question is not doubting the power of the Word of God. It is simply recognizing that the Spirit can work through a variety of means in which the Word is proclaimed. Sometimes that proclamation can take place more effectively in interpersonal involvement in small groups. At times it may take place in an action program.

One way some churches are developing a greater discipline is by having all their members formally renew their membership every year. Instead of going on the assumption that once a member of a congregation, always a member until you disassociate yourself from it, it suggests that each year every member take the initiative of stating whether the church means enough to him that he wants to stay in. If he does not take that initiative, that is pretty good evidence that the church did not mean very much to him. This approach may result in smaller but more dedicated memberships.

Some congregations are adopting a covenant that every member signs and must renew each year if he wishes to continue his membership. In some congregations this covenant has indeed become the "working constitution" and a separate document forms the legal constitution, which contains only the bare essentials required by law.

The following covenant was adopted by a congregation of The American Lutheran Church, the Church of the Covenant, Carson, California:

PREAMBLE

Seeking to express our commitment to Jesus Christ as Lord and to be God's instruments in his world, feeling the need to draw together in community to share our Christian life and stance of servanthood; and desiring to enter a wider fellowship of believers through the American Lutheran Church, we, collectively and individually, enter into this covenant with God and each other.

1. To become a vital, contributing member of a koinonia group.

2. To participate in a minimum of one retreat every six months.

3. To be responsible for preparation of and participation in Sunday worship.

4. To become aware that the changing needs, moods and currents of the world require constant re-examination of our methods of ministry; to perform our ministry in our daily lives through work, leisure, family and neighbors as responsible Christians.

5. To give a significant portion of our time, talents and resources toward the ongoing mission of the church, with a tithe as a goal.

6. To accept God and each other, unconditionally, in love with both honesty and gentleness.

7. To make strangers feel genuinely welcome so that the gift of community and promise of the Gospel might be shared.

8. To meet God through prayer and study.

From the beginning the congregation has objected to the idea of a church building that would sit empty much of the time. At the time of this writing they are thinking in terms of a community-use type building. Or, they may decide to use existing church buildings at an "unholy" hour when not in use by the owner.

What worked in Carson, California, may not work everywhere, and it probably is not desirable that it should. For while the style of church life in this Church of the Covenant has some very exciting aspects, it probably cannot provide some of the other dimensions of the Christian life that are also very meaningful. The congregation may remain comparatively small in size, and that in itself is not bad. Some tasks can probably be done better by a number of small groups than by one large group. The smaller congregation, however, will miss one experience that a larger congregation can have, and that is the distinctive kind of celebration that comes in large groups. Perhaps that is why Mr. Tapp predicted that in the next 25 years it will become acceptable for people to belong to more than one church, so they can have a variety of meaningful experiences.

The covenant approach has some exciting possibilities. While it might be argued that the more traditional forms used for reception of members into a congregation includes many of these same elements, the pointedness and relevance of the covenant language makes it refreshingly practical.

There are also some problems connected with the covenant approach, and those congregations that use it should at least be aware of them. If we use the analogy that a church is like a hospital to which sick people go for cure, then a quick reading of the covenant would lead you to believe that the church in Carson is only for the spiritually mature. One could use the covenant as a legalistic screen to keep out what in traditional language is called dead wood or inactive members.

We have made a mistake in the past when we have allowed these people to think that going to church several times a year, contributing a few dollars and going to communion once a year keeps them on the church rolls and thus "members in good standing." On the other hand, churches must show a real concern for these people. As long as one is aware of the dangers of the covenant approach, it still seems to be far better than anything that is in second place.

One strength of the covenant approach is the emphasis it places on responsible concern for others. Two programs that have become widespread throughout the country are known as FISH and SWITCHBOARD. The programs are similar in that they provide the mechanics with which someone in need can call a number and be placed in touch with someone who can help—hence, the name SWITCHBOARD.

An increasing number of churches are adding a position to their staff known as director of volunteer services. As indicated earlier, most congregations are structured excellently to fulfill one of the functions of the church, nurturing the faith of members through worship and education. They are not so well structured to serve the community. Yet there are usually many individuals in a congregation who are glad to render some kind of service, but there is a gap between their willingness and the structure with which they can carry it out. A part or full-time director of volunteer services may be the first step in developing such a structure. He or she can direct the talents and interests of people into those channels where they can be used.

A basic first step for any congregation that wants to design new structures is to state goals and objectives in precise, even measurable terms. There is nothing wrong with such a broad objective as "proclamation of the gospel." It is so broad, however, that it has lost some of its meaning. A congregation would indeed be proclaiming the gospel if it held church services every Sunday at which portions of the Bible were expounded. But it might engender much more enthusiasm if it set for itself a more precise, limited sub-goal, such as: this year we're going to concentrate on making our worship more meaningful.

While at first glance this too may seem quite general, it can be made specific so that at the end of the year you can really tell whether you have achieved your objective. Despite our earlier reference to measuring everything in terms of numbers, there is something numbers can tell you. If during this year your attendance keeps going down, it at least gives you opportunity to ask the question "why?" And if it goes up, you need to examine the means by which the increase was effected. If you used a competitive program of awards to improve attendance, you haven't really accomplished very much.

One way to achieve greater interest in worship is to conduct a number of workshops on worship. If during a year a hundred people read one or more books on worship, if there is a general increase in enthusiasm and participation in worship, and if there are other tangible and intangible ways in which your congregation has become more appreciative of the meaning and importance of worship, then you have reason to believe you achieved your objective.

Or, a congregation may decide that its objective for a given year shall be to become more aware of the concerns of the world and the responsibility of the church to become involved in these concerns. It can then set up specific ways in which this can be accomplished, such as special projects, personal involvement other than just giving money, and intensive study groups. At the end of the year it should evaluate how successfully it has achieved its objective.

Too often congregations make the mistake of thinking that they have to do everything and that it is a sin to say no to requests. The consequences of not designing a specific program can be doing many things superficially and nothing really well.

There is no easy way of designing an adequate program, but without one, a congregation loses its sense of purpose. It may even lose its life, even though it continues going through the forms and mechanics of having weekly meetings. It will most certainly lose its sense of excitement, and if there is anything Christianity should be, it's exciting.

The challenge of a council or committee member is to help revitalize a church. You can help make it happen.

As an opener for moving a listless council or congregation into the first steps of an exciting discovery of its own potential, try this experiment at an evening gathering.

Call it a mixer if you will, and tell the group that for a half hour they are to mix and engage in general conversation, but that at the end of the half hour they are to have divided themselves into two groups. There are no rigid rules as to how they arrive in these two groups. There is to be no counting off into one, two, one, two. Each is to gravitate into the group in which he feels most comfortable.

Then at the end of the half hour, give this assignment: your congregation has just been given $100,000. Spend the next half hour in a discussion of how you think the other group would spend the $100,000.

You will be in for an evening of intergroup dynamics you won't soon forget.

8

DON'T BURN DOWN A CATHEDRAL TO FRY AN EGG

The previous chapter may come as heady wine and stir the adrenalin of a progressive young layman who is chafing at the bit and wants to swing into action to make his church relevant. He will have little problem if he is a part of a group of like-minded people who are starting a mission where at present there is no church. Those who aren't interested in this kind of church simply won't join the group.

But if this progressive layman is a member of an established congregation with a long history, he is likely to meet frustration. Chances are that not everybody will be intrigued with his idea. Now what does he do? Does he leave and join a group more in tune with his thinking? Does he polarize groups within his church? How fast does he move?

One person said it this way, "Don't burn down a cathedral to fry an egg." Roland Tapp may be 100 percent correct when he says that "there will be no more projects for building huge church plants," but what do you do with church buildings now in existence? Obviously you don't burn them down.

But what kind of imagination can you come up with that will make the most of what is on hand? This need not refer only to church buildings, but can refer as well to organizational patterns that have acquired sanctity through the years, whether they have deserved it or not.

Keith Miller in his book, *The Taste of New Wine,* entitles the last chapter, "What about the Old Wine-skins?" He describes the experience of some who after years of finding the church rather dull suddenly become electrified. But when they try to carry this enthusiasm back to the church, instead of being received with equal enthusiasm, they are rejected, or at most given a cold shoulder. What can be done when a person would like to inject new life into an institution only to find that the institution prefers death or at most irrelevance?

Miller says, "I do not agree with those who have 'given up' on the institutional church, as difficult as the situation sometimes seems to be to ministers and laymen. I think there is a way. The new wine will not burst the old wineskins if the handlers of the old wineskins will receive the new wine and pour it quickly into new skins themselves. This is already happening in many places. And where it is, churches are coming alive with new and deeper involvement with God in his contemporary redeeming activity. Men and women are being reborn to new purpose and loyalty in Christ's love. Such churches are becoming centers for small groups of struggling Christians to come together for worship and training. Many are finding totally new meaning in the sacraments and the Word."

Richard E. Byrd, a former Episcopal rector and now president of Jones and Byrd, Inc., a Minneapolis consulting firm, has devised a scale for organizational creativity and risk-taking to help a congregation determine the degree of innovation it is willing to undertake.

The scale is based on the simple principle that as the ideas get more "far out" the risk goes up.

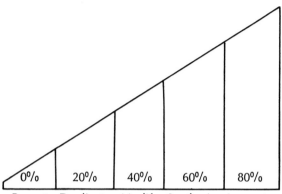

| 0% | 20% | 40% | 60% | 80% |
| Repeat | Duplicate | Modify | Synthesize | Innovate |

If your purpose is to avoid all risk, the best procedure is simply to repeat what you did last year. That's probably the reason the favorite statement in many congregations is, "We've always done it this way." Repetition demands no creativity. Very seldom does anything exciting happen in these congregations; but then neither does anything go wrong very often. They do things the way they have always been done. There's no risk involved. Sometimes you can live for a long time that way. Volkswagen has done it for many years with unbelievable success. But even it is changing, and the next diagram will tell you why.

Always using exactly the same form of worship at the same hour without any variation are examples of repetition. So also are using the same Sunday school teachers year after year without questioning their effectiveness from time to time, or using exactly the same form of opening service for Sunday school.

A step up the scale of creativity is duplication. A congregation sees a program another church has tried and simply duplicates it. There is reason to think it will work because it has already worked elsewhere. But the situation could be different, so there is a little risk involved. Byrd sets that risk at 20%. Duplication is slightly more creative, and therefore also slightly more risky than mere repetition.

A congregation that modifies a program that has been tried elsewhere injects more creativity, for it departs from the completely tried and tested by modifying it to something that has not been done before. The risk goes up to 40%.

Synthesizing is up the risk-taking scale another 20% to 60%. A congregation that synthesizes is quite creative and progressive. It has probably had an active leadership group that have tried to keep abreast of the times. Some members of this group may have gone to workshops where new ideas were discussed and practiced. They have read books by progressive churchmen. From these various sources they have picked up ideas here and there and put them together in a new program for their church. Probably no other church has ever tried a program quite like this. Consequently the risk is greater.

The highest element of risk comes in innovating an original, new program that has never been tried before. These don't happen very often either in the religious or secular world. One brand new innovation every 10 years is a high average. The airplane, for instance, was an innovation, but from the time that the Wright Brothers flew the Kitty Hawk until the day of the first jet plane, all improvements were modifications or syntheses of known principles. The jet engine, the computer, Xerox were innovations.

Innovations in the religious world may include such things as the Roman Catholic Church giving up Latin in the service. Radical changes in worship services in any church involve a high risk factor.

We have been talking about short-range risk factors in organizational creativity. In other words a church that is constantly introducing innovative programs runs a high risk of losing a lot of members. Byrd points out, however, that for long range planning, the scale for organizational creativity and risk-taking reverses itself.

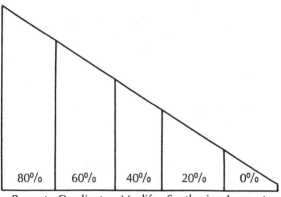

In other words, while repeating last year's program may have a 0% risk factor if you are interested in preserving the church merely one more year, it has an 80% risk factor over the long haul. A congregation that never makes any changes, that does everything the same this year as it did last year, may not die immediately, but eventually it will die. Even Volkswagen is learning that. It was able to live for a long time by repeating last year's model. It knows it can't continue living that way.

On the other hand a congregation that courageously does the right things, even though they may be highly innovative and cause members to leave, may have a good, long future—if the innovative things they do are indeed right.

The big question is how innovative should you be? How big a risk should you take? Even the best Christian is not spared from fallibility. Two Christians, equally dedicated in their Christian commitment and equally intelligent may have differing views on procedures to reach a goal on which both may agree.

Willingness to take risks does not mean to throw caution and common sense to the wind. Wisdom would not dictate that all of a congregation's programs should be in the 80% risk category. It's quite possible that a number of things done last year should be repeated this year, thus reducing the overall risk element.

One tactic to avoid risk even for innovative programs is to point out that perhaps they are just a return to old programs. For instance, the current emphasis on small groups and house churches is not all that innovative. It is really a repetition or duplication of the early New Testament practices.

In addition to common sense and caution, there is no substitute for love and concern. One night members of a congregation that had a nationwide reputation for innovation were debating as to whether they were really open to people. It seemed almost a rhetorical question. Wasn't their very progressiveness evidence that they were indeed open to new ideas and to people?

But one very perceptive member observed: "No, I don't think we are as open as we think we are. We are open to those to the left of us. But are we really open to those on the right of us?"

No group of people has a corner on bigotry. Conservatives are traditionally noted for their lack of openness to people with ideas contrary to their own. But liberals can be just as guilty of being totally closed to those who are not as liberal as they are.

The last chapter, "You Do It by Doing It," will give more practical helps on how to walk that tight rope of not compromising oneself for fear of losing a few members. In other words, to the chapter title, "Don't Burn Down the Cathedral to Fry an Egg," must be added the question whether a proposed action would indeed be burning down the cathedral.

Scales for organizational creativity and risk taking used in this chapter are copyrighted by Richard E. Byrd and are used with his permission.

9

GETTING ALONG
WITH
THE PASTOR
AND
THE CHURCH AT LARGE

Perhaps a more diplomatic title could have been found for this chapter. It seems to imply that there is a triangular involvement of misunderstanding among members of a congregation, the pastor, and denominational headquarters. Sometimes that's true.

It seems to imply that the pastor is hard to get along with. Sometimes that's true too. And if it is, it is not always the fault of the pastor. Sometimes it's the fault of the parishioners. A congregation can be hard to get along with too. And sometimes it's merely the result of changing circumstances. The role of the pastor in American life is changing, and in some places neither pastor nor congregation have fully acclimated themselves to the change.

There was a time when the pastor, the doctor, and the school teacher were the most highly educated people in the community. The pastor was highly respected and looked to with some sense of awe. He supposedly had the answers to questions—even in matters other than theology—and people came to him for these answers. But times have changed. The pastor is the first to admit that there are many in his congregation more highly educated than he. His role is changing from that of an answer man to that of stimulating his people to ask the right questions.

We could have quite a debate as to who put the pastor in the answer man position in the first place. Many times the members of a congregation much prefer a minister who makes decisions for them. It's much easier to spot a wrong answer and second-guess the one who gave it and even castigate him for it than to struggle with difficult questions yourself and assume some of the responsibility for making a mistake.

On the other hand, ministers too are human; and it takes a strong sense of identity and security to be thrown into a position where for an hour a week he has the complete attention of his entire congregation, even the mantle of being a spokesman for God, and then to face the fact that his real task is to enable and free others to "do their thing" instead of "doing his own thing."

Keith Miller in *The Taste of New Wine*, describes an episode that points out the humanity of pastor as well as parishioner. A woman who had been a loyal churchgoer for years had suddenly had an experience outside the church to vitalize her faith. In her joy she went to tell her pastor, thinking that he too would be overjoyed.

Not only was he not overjoyed; his response was rather grim and frowning. Without excusing him, Miller tries to rationalize the minister's reaction. He was a successful minister with a theological degree from a large and academically respectable divinity school. He had preached and performed his parish functions faithfully throughout the years. And now comes this woman who, after exposure to all this, claims that the real vitalization of her Christian faith was sparked by someone outside the church, not even theologically trained. From the minister's perspective, his parishioner seemed to be saying that he missed the boat completely. His security was threatened.

On the other hand, the parishioner might have used a better approach. She might have thanked the minister for remaining faithful while she was going through the "dry years" of her own religious experience and upholding her in his prayers.

The issue is mostly one of understanding. And if ever there is an institution that ought to know how to deal with misunderstandings, it should be the church. That's what the doctrine of forgiveness, one of the major doctrines of the church, is all about.

Too often there is a we-you attitude between pastor and parishioners or a we-they attitude between parishioners and members of a church council or committee. The first principle for harmonious relations is for pastor and committee and congregation all to think in terms of we. We-they thinking should be outlawed in the church.

This does not mean that there will never be raised voices in debate, but it does mean that there should be a maturity that allows for give and take, the freedom to challenge opinions, and the willingness to have one's own opinions challenged and scrutinized.

The relationship between a congregation and the denomination's national office also is sometimes one of misunderstanding. Some congregations tend to think that the main function of denominational headquarters is to impose programs on local congregations and extract funds from them.

There can be a healthy tension between a congregation and the denominational headquarters. Congregations are in danger of thinking too parochially. They have a tendency to see concerns close at hand and be oblivious to the larger programs. Denominational offices, on the other hand, can become so engrossed in vast programs that they lose concern for the congregation's local program and see a congregation only as a means to the end of meeting the national budget.

An illustration of this was evident at a recent conference of pastors when one denominational executive said of a speaker, who was a pastor of the denomination, "I'll really be interested in what he has to say. His congregation has the poorest benevolence record of anyone in our whole church." That was the one fact he knew about that man, and on that fact he had based an opinion on him and his congregation.

We are in for some drastic rethinking of congregation-denomination relationships. Major denominational treasuries are on the downswing at a time when congregational offerings are holding their own and going up. Congregations want to have a greater hand in determining how their money will be used.

Some congregations are starting foundations of their own, not to guarantee a future for their own life but to enable them to be mobile enough to swing into action and support a variety of projects.

The minister of one congregation that hopes to build a foundation of a million dollars said, "There are some things that a local congregation can do better than a national church body and other things that a national church body can obviously do better than a local church. We feel the time is ripe for our members to respond to a program of this kind. Our intention is to put our money—even some of our capital if the project is worthy—into seed-money programs, to help something get started. Projects should be able to grow on their own once they have gotten started. If we subsidize something for a second year, it will be on a decreasing basis."

Programs of this magnitude used to be done only by national church bodies. Now that some of the larger congregations are starting them, fully aware of some of the dangers of proliferation, it would be unfortunate if competition or mistrust developed. Every congregation might well have a committee of denominational relationships which would engage in a continuing conversation with the denominational headquarters on new and dynamic programs, some to be carried out by the congregation and others by the congregation in coordination with other congregations through a national program.

Seldom has the church been faced with as many exciting potentials in interpersonal relationships between pastor and parishioners and between congregation and denomination. There can be misunderstandings and hard feelings, but there can also be challenges undreamed of in earlier generations.

You as a council or committee member can help make it happen by participating in this dynamic interchange.

10

YOU
DO
IT
BY
DOING IT

There are some rather dynamic verses in the Gospel of John that Phillips translates in this way: Jesus went up to the Temple and began teaching. The Jews were amazed and remarked, "How does this man know all this—he has never been taught?"

Jesus replied to them: "My teaching is not really mine but comes from the one who sent me. **If anyone wants to do God's will, he will know** whether my teaching is from God or whether I merely speak on my own authority."

The point he was making was that you find out how valid an idea is by putting it into practice. The implication for our purposes here is that there comes a time when you no longer debate the merits of a plan. You get to work on it. You do it by doing it. In other words, the time for discussion is over. The time for action is here.

You will have observed that this book has been quite short on giving specific suggestions on how to do things. There was a reason for this. We go on the assumption that average congregations have many more resources for creative programs than they give themselves credit for. Too often they think they have to pay an outside expert to come in and give them ideas. But the expert will know that all he can really do is free them from inhibitions so that they are not afraid to put their imagination to use.

At a recent meeting of ministers and laymen where a consultant made this very point, a young lady testified, "I really believe that. I experienced it myself. My husband told me—very kindly but very objectively—that I wasn't creative enough to carry off a certain project. I decided to show him. Though I had never made a flower arrangement in my life, I entered 10 flower arrangements in an exhibit and I came back with eight blue ribbons."

We are afraid to try things because we are afraid we will fail. We resist change because we think change is bad or at least too risky. We may not be totally happy with what we have but we at least know what we have. We can't be sure that if we change, things will be better. We look at change as losing something we had instead of gaining something new.

Paradoxically, the church has been at least partially responsible for our resistance to change by the hymns we sing, by the slogans we coin, and by the Scripture passages we quote at the exclusion of others. For instance, every time we sing, "Change and decay in all around I see; O thou who changest not, abide with me," we are saying change is bad. Every time we comfort ourselves with the slogan, "a changeless Christ for a changing world," we are implying that change is less desirable than change-lessness. Every time we emphasize, "Jesus Christ, the same yesterday, today and forever," without awareness of some other Scripture passages we are saying there is something intrinsically bad about change.

The fact is that the Bible also has some positive things to say about change. It also says, "Old things are passed away; all things have become new." It speaks of new wineskins for new wine. The very concept of pilgrimage—a very Christian term—implies change, going from somewhere to somewhere.

If only we could really take the doctrine of grace at full face value, we would be freed to try new things. Grace forgives our mistakes; it encourages us to try new things. Abraham could have played it safe and spent the rest of his life in Ur of the Chaldees. He might have had a much safer life there, but think of all the exciting adventure with God he would have missed.

Too often we go on the assumption that we are all alone in wanting to change things. We underestimate others, who may be longing for change just as much as we are and who may be hungering for the fellowship of others to join them in innovation. True, a vast majority may be timid about changes, and they should not be criticized too sharply for that is only human nature. But it could be that among this majority there are a half dozen or a dozen or two who are waiting for someone with the courage to lead and they will gladly follow.

You may be the one they are waiting for. You can help make it happen.

READINGS

Following is a suggested bibliography, intended to stimulate church councilmen or prospective church councilmen to get into the exciting arena of church renewal. Recommending a book does not necessarily mean agreeing with all that is in it, nor does recommending this series of books suggest that you ought to try everything that is recommended in them. Least of all does it mean that once an author has suggested something, he is willing to live by it for the rest of his life himself. For instance, Colin Williams, author of *What in the World?* and *Where in the World?,* two books listed below, is reported to have said that he takes a different view today than he did when he wrote these books. Nevertheless the books provide stimulation for new thinking. It should be taken for granted that every member of a church council should read at least a few books every year in the area of church life. The following list is a good beginning:

RENEWAL AND MISSION

Abbot, Walter M. The Documents of Vatican II. New York: Association Press, 1966.

Rose, Stephen C. The Grass Roots Church. Nashville: Abingdon Press, 1966.

Weber, Hans-Reudi. Salty Christians. New York: Seabury Press, 1963.

Williams, Colin. What in the World? New York: Department of Publication Services, National Council of Churches of Christ in the USA, 1964.

Where in the World? New York: Department of Publication Services, National Council of Churches of Christ in the USA, 1963.

THE CHURCHES AND CHANGING SOCIETY

Cox, Harvey. The Secular City. New York: The Macmillan Company, 1965.

Doxiadis, Constantinos and Douglass, Truman B. The New World of Urban Man. Philadelphia: United Church Press, 1965.

Hadden, Jeffrey K. The Gathering Storm in the Churches. New York: Doubleday, 1969.

Moseley, J. Brooke. Christians in the Technical and Social Revolutions. From the report of the 1966 World Conference on Church and Society, held in Geneva and sponsored by the World Council of Churches.

Shinn, Roger. Tangled World. *New York: Charles Scribner's Sons, 1965.*

Winter, Gibson. The New Creation as Metropolis. *New York: The Macmillan Company, 1963.*

The Suburban Captivity of the Churches. *New York: The Macmillan Company, 1961.*

MINISTRY AND LAITY

Come, Arnold B. Agents of Reconciliation. *Philadelphia: The Westminster Press. Revised and enlarged edition.*

Congar, Y. M. J. Lay People in the Church. *Glen Rock, N.J.: Newman Press. Revised edition.*

Gibbs, Mark and Morton, T. Ralph. God's Frozen People. *Philadelphia: The Westminster Press, 1964.*

Grimes, Howard. The Rebirth of the Laity. *Nashville: Abingdon Press, 1965.*

Halvorson, Loren E. Exodus into the World. *Minneapolis: Augsburg, 1966.*

Miller, Keith. The Taste of New Wine. *Waco, Tex.: Word Books, 1965.*

A Second Touch. *Waco, Tex.: Word Books, 1967.*

Neill, Stephen Charles and Weber, Hans-Reudi, eds. The Layman in Christian History. *Philadelphia: Westminster Press, 1963.*

Robinson, J. A. T. *The New Reformation?* Philadelphia: The Westminster Press, 1965.

Stringfellow, William. *A Private and Public Faith.* Grand Rapids, Mich.: William B. Eerdmanns, 1962.

Trueblood, Elton. *The Company of the Committed.* New York: Harper and Row, 1961.

Date Due